The
HEALTHY BODY
BOOK

Caring for the Coolest Machine You'll Ever Own

by Ellen Sabin

and _____

WRITE YOUR NAME HERE

WATERING CAN® PRESS
www.wateringcanpress.com

WATERING CAN®

Growing Kids with Character

When you care about things and nurture them,
they will grow healthy, strong, and happy, and in turn,
they will make the world a better place.

All Watering Can Press titles are available at special quantity discounts for bulk purchases
for sales promotion, premiums, fund-raising, educational, or institutional use.

Watering Can Press offers customized versions of this book and will adjust content for use
by nonprofits and corporations in support of their community outreach and marketing goals.

**To inquire about bulk discounts or to learn more about customized book runs,
please visit our Web site or e-mail info@wateringcanpress.com.**

Text and illustrations © 2009 by Ellen Sabin
WATERING CAN is a registered trademark of Ellen Sabin.
Watering Can, New York, NY
Printed in China in January 2015

Written by Ellen Sabin
Illustrated by Kerren Barbas
Designed by Taryn Sefecka

ISBN-978-0-9759868-8-2

Web site address: www.wateringcanpress.com

Dear _____,

Because you are such an amazing, caring, and responsible person, I am giving you this **HEALTHY BODY BOOK**.

In this book, you'll learn about your incredible body. You will discover how it works and all of the remarkable things that it can do.

Along the way, you'll also find out about ways you can care for your body to keep it strong and healthy.

As you go through this book, you will see that you—and your decisions—are powerful. Your choices can make a BIG difference in how you feel and how healthy you can be.

From, _____

Some "thank-yous"

- To my parents for helping and inspiring me—something they do in nearly all of my endeavors. I see them bike, ski, hike, or walk every day. They enjoy, and take care of, their bodies, and they have passed along that value to me.

- Samantha, Taryn, and Kerren add their incredible talents to my books, and I value them all. I also thank George, Josh, and Courtney for their ever-present behind-the-scenes support of Watering Can Press.

- Thanks to the health care experts who reviewed the content of this book for accuracy, the parents who read assorted drafts for tone, and the kids who helped me find fun ways to teach about health.

- A special thanks to Sydney, my six-year-old niece, for reminding me to add the very important section on moderation!

A NOTE TO ADULTS

The HEALTHY BODY BOOK is meant to inspire children to grow
a deeper understanding and respect for their bodies.

In turn, they'll come to appreciate their bodies' gifts, learn about
their bodies' needs, and do things to maintain their health . . . not just
because it's "good for them," but because they WANT to!

Along the way, this activity book will help them learn about their bodies,
see the power of their actions to make a difference in their health, practice
responsibility by making healthy choices, and enhance their sense of self-worth.

Ultimately, I hope The HEALTHY BODY BOOK journey will help
inspire children toward forming habits that will have a positive impact
on their health and well-being throughout their lives.

Table of Contents

● **What Is The HEALTHY BODY BOOK?** 6
    Here's How It Works . . .

● **Introducing the Incredible, Amazing, Fantastic YOU!** . . 10

● **Your BODY** 20
    Peek Inside and Learn about the Systems That Make It Work

● **Being a FRIEND to Your Body** 30
    What Does Your Body Need from You?

● **Healthy HABITS** 40
    . . . For a Healthy You!

● **SPEAK UP for Health!** 50

● **Other Stuff** 58

Welcome to Your **HEALTHY BODY BOOK!**

Did you know that YOU—and the decisions you make—will have a HUGE effect on how healthy you are today, tomorrow, and for your entire life?

Your body is incredible, and it needs **you** to make healthy choices to keep it strong, safe, and working.

The HEALTHY BODY BOOK is all about you.

As you read this book, you will see that your body is a good friend to you, and that you can be a good friend back to your body, too.

> ### Just like a good friend, your body gives you many special and important things.
>
> - It allows you to move around in all sorts of ways.
> - It lets you enjoy sounds, sights, smells, tastes, and touches.
> - It fights off illness.
> - It has a brain that gives you imagination, memories, dreams, and more.

Well, friends take care of each other, right?

The HEALTHY BODY BOOK will help you find ways to be a good friend back to your body!

What are you waiting for? Turn the page and get started!

How does
The HEALTHY BODY BOOK work?

First You get to learn about the most amazing machine in the world—your body!

Next You learn what your body needs to be healthy.

Then You think about the things that you want to do to care for your body.

And You get to DO THINGS—all sorts of things—to help yourself stay healthy, strong, and happy.

Then You get to do these things OVER and OVER and OVER again, and make being as healthy as possible a daily part of your life.

It's that easy!

REMEMBER: This is YOUR book. Along the way, you can fill in the blanks, draw pictures, and collect ideas about all of the ways you can make choices that are good for your body.

Introducing the Incredible, Amazing, Fantastic YOU!

This book is all about your body.

Your body is the most amazing and most complicated machine in the entire world!

Many machines have just one job. A car gets you from one place to another. An oven cooks food. A radio plays music.

But, unlike these machines that are designed to do one thing, your body can do MANY different things. You can make it walk, jump, talk, solve math problems, and much, much, more.

You can even make it do more than one thing at a time. There's no other machine in the world that can do everything your body can do!

Your body is so amazing that it can even do things without you telling it to do them. Every minute of every day, your body is working hard in many ways.

Your body is very complicated, and it is also unique. On the outside, your body looks different from every other person in the whole world. That makes it pretty special!

So turn the page and start thinking about the coolest machine you'll ever own—*your body.*

How Your Body Looks on the Outside

Even though people are made up of the same parts on the outside
(eyes, nose, mouth, hair, skin, arms, legs), we all look different.

Some people have blue eyes, while others have brown eyes.
Some people have light skin, while others have darker skin.
Some people are tall, while others are shorter.

However you look is great, because it makes you look like . . . YOU!

Draw a picture of yourself here.

No one else in the whole world looks just like you.
That makes you very special and unique!

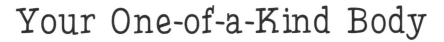

Your One-of-a-Kind Body

The reason people look different from one another
is because of their **genes.**

Our bodies are made up of trillions of tiny cells. Inside those tiny cells
are bits of information called genes. Genes give instructions to your body.
They tell your body how to grow and how to work.

Your genes were passed to you by your mother and father before you were
born. No one in the world has the exact same mix of genes as you . . . not
even your brothers and sisters (unless you are an identical twin!).

Another one-of-a-kind part of your body is your fingerprint.
Did you know that while you were growing inside of your mother,
you already had your fingerprint? No two people in the world
have the exact same fingerprint.

Let's see yours!

Ask an adult to help you put your thumbprint in the box below.

Incredible Machines . . . Yours Is the Coolest!

Machines can do some amazing things, but your body can do even more!

Some machines, like cars or scooters, can move from place to place.

But your body can run, jump, flip, bend, and move in more ways than any machine ever made.

Some machines, like calculators, can do really hard math. Others, like TVs, make pictures that you can see.

Your body has a brain that can think, make decisions, learn new things, imagine, remember, and do stuff that's more complicated than even the smartest computer.

Some machines, like voice-activated cell phones, can use hearing.

Your body can see, smell, feel, taste, AND hear things. It uses all five senses to help you experience the world.

Machines need help when they break down or get damaged. Mechanics fix cars, plumbers fix pipes, and electricians fix lights.

Your body can heal itself. Sometimes doctors help people when their bodies are hurt, but your body also has its own ways to fight off illness and repair itself.

What Your Body Can Do

Your body can do so many different things.
Circle the things that you can do.

swim   run   jump

wink   TALK   wiggle your toes

sing   climb a tree   smell flowers

snowboard   taste an apple

hear music   laugh   play an instrument

dream

DO A CARTWHEEL

do a sit-up   skate   whistle

RIDE A BIKE   dance

feel a hug   sew

Having Fun Moving Around

Below, draw a picture or paste a photo of yourself having fun and moving around.

You can show yourself playing a sport, taking a walk with your family,
going on vacation, swimming in the sea, or anything else you can think of.

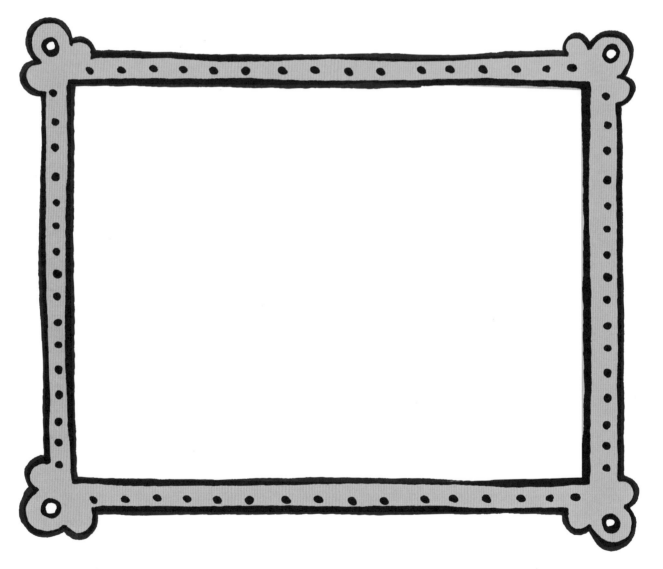

When your body is strong and healthy, it lets you move around,
play, do sports, and have lots of fun with your friends and family.

Enjoying Your Senses

People use their senses to experience the world.
The five senses are seeing, hearing, tasting, smelling, and feeling.

Seeing the words in a book allows you to read great stories. What is your favorite book?

....

....

Hearing a song might make you want to dance. List your three favorite songs:

1 ....

2 ....

3 ....

Tasting yummy food can make your mouth water. List your favorite foods:

....

....

....

Smelling sweet flowers can make you feel good or bring back nice memories. What is your favorite smell and why?

....

....

Feeling a soft blanket can make you want to snuggle up in bed. List some things that feel nice to touch:

....

....

Besides giving you great experiences, your senses are also really important because they can help keep you safe. You can see a walk signal on the street and know when to cross. You can hear a lifeguard's whistle when there is danger. You can smell smoke when there is a fire. You can taste when food has spoiled. You can feel pain when you touch a hot stove.

Your body uses your senses to let you enjoy things and to keep you safe every day. THANKS, senses!

Your Body Can Learn to Do New Things

In addition to all the things that you can make your body do today, there are lots of other things that it can learn to do in the future.

Maybe you want to learn to dive off a diving board, do a backflip in gymnastics, hit a home run, or play the piano.

Write down some things you want to learn to do.

....

....

....

....

Can you think of any other machine that learns how to do new things?

It's Working All the Time

You just thought about lots of things that you can tell your body to do. But did you know that your body is so amazing that it can do things without you even thinking about it?

For example, your heart is beating and your lungs are breathing every minute of every day. And when you get a cut or have a cold, your body goes into action and does things to heal itself.

Even when you're asleep, your body is still working.

What are you THANKFUL for?

People rarely think about all of the great things their bodies let them do.

We all have special skills and talents that make us unique.
Maybe you are great at soccer, playing the violin, or spelling.
Maybe you have a great memory or you know how to speak two languages.

Below, you can list some of your skills and talents that you are
thankful your body and mind allow you to do.

1. ....

2. ....

3. ....

4. ....

5. ....

6. ....

7. ....

8. ....

9. ....

10. ....

It looks like your body deserves a big THANK YOU!

YOUR BODY

Peek Inside and Learn about the Systems That Make It Work

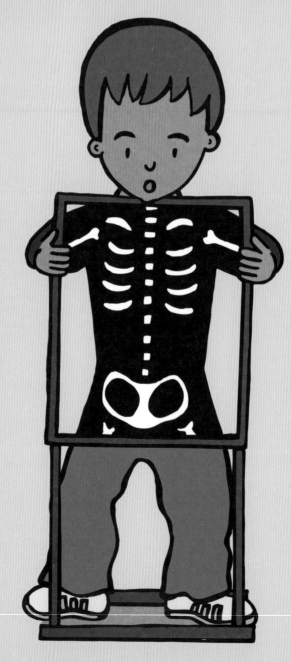

Your body is very complicated, and also very smart.

It is made up of many small parts that each has its own job. These parts are constantly working together to make your body function.

If you could peek inside your body, what would you find?

- Very small parts inside your body are called **cells**. You have trillions of cells. They have different shapes and sizes and many different jobs. Cells are so small that 500 of them would fit in the period at the end of this sentence.

- When a group of similar cells come together, they form **tissue**. Skin, bones, muscles, and fat are all kinds of tissue.

- When different kinds of tissue work together, they can form an **organ**. Your heart, lungs, eyes, and brain are examples of organs. Organs do things to keep your body working.

- Organs work together in special ways to operate **systems**. Systems control things like your breathing, thinking, movement, and other body functions.

Some examples of systems in your body are:

the dermal system
(your skin)

the skeletal system
(your bones)

the digestive system
(how you process food)

the immune system
(how you fight off illness)

the nervous system
(your feelings and reflexes)

the respiratory system
(your breathing)

the cardiovascular system
(your heart and blood)

On the next pages, you can begin to explore these systems.

Your Dermal System

Main job: To cover and protect your body.

About: This system is made up mostly of skin, but also includes hair, nails, and sweat and oil glands. Skin is your body's outside covering. It's waterproof, like a raincoat, so when your skin gets wet, water slides off of it. Skin protects your body by keeping things like sunlight, dirt, and germs out. It also keeps your muscles, bones, and organs inside your body where they belong.

Did you know? There are three main layers of skin. The epidermis is the thin

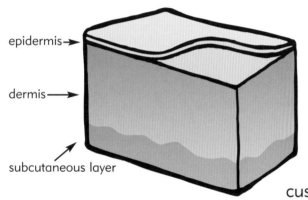

epidermis→

dermis→

subcutaneous layer

outside layer of skin that you can see. It's tough and strong and very good at protecting your body. The dermis is the middle layer of your skin. It is stretchy and contains nerves and blood vessels. The nerves in your skin let you feel things—like if it is hot or cold outside or if something feels soft or hard. The third layer of skin is called the subcutaneous layer. This layer of skin has a lot of cushioning and protects you if you fall. It also acts like a blanket and helps to keep you warm.

Your body is SO smart that . . . When you get a cut, your skin repairs itself! It makes a scab. A scab is like your own homemade bandage that prevents germs from getting inside your body.

Fun facts:

● Skin is flexible so you can bend. As you grow, skin stretches and grows with you.

● On hot days, your skin helps you cool off by releasing heat from your body in the form of sweat. On cold days, your skin keeps heat inside of you.

Your Skeletal System

About: The skeletal system is made up of bones, ligaments, and tendons. Bones give structure to your body so that you can move in all sorts of different ways. Ligaments connect bones to each other, and tendons connect bones to your muscles. Since bones are hard, they also protect the organs inside your body. For example, the bones that make up your rib cage form a shield to protect your heart, lungs, and liver. Your skull bones acts like a helmet to protect your brain.

Did you know? Bones are alive. They are made up of trillions of living cells which help them to grow.

Your body is SO smart that . . . Bones don't bend, but they can move in different directions thanks to your joints. Joints are the places where two bones come together. Some joints can move back and forth like door hinges, and others can twist or swing. You have joints in your elbows, knees, wrists, hips, and other places.

Fun facts:

- A baby's body has about 300 bones. An adult has 206. That's because some bones grow together as you get older.

- The longest bone in your body is your thigh bone (called the femur). It's about 1/4 of your height.

- The smallest bone in your body is the stirrup bone. It's inside your ear.

- Bones are also a storage place (like a closet) for some of the minerals—such as calcium—that your body needs to be strong. When your body needs calcium, it gets it from your bones.

Your Digestive System

Main job: To turn food you eat into energy for your body.

About: Just as a car needs fuel like gasoline to move, your body needs fuel to give it energy. Food is your fuel, and your digestive system is what turns food into energy.

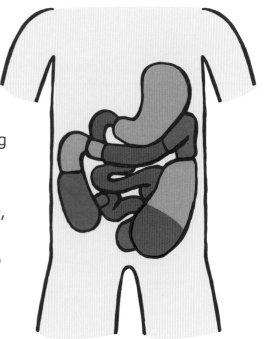

Did you know? Here's how food becomes energy: First, you chew your food into small pieces and then you swallow it. Next, it gets pushed down a tube called the esophagus and lands in your stomach. There it gets squeezed and mixed up until it becomes like a thick soup. Then it travels through a long tube called your small intestine, where it is mixed with digestive juices and squished up even more until it's as thin as a liquid. As it travels through your small intestine, your food is broken down into nutrients. These nutrients pass through the walls of the small intestine and go into your blood. The blood then carries the nutrients to all parts of your body to give you energy to work, play, and grow.

Your body is SO smart that . . . Your body knows what it needs from food. It keeps the parts that it needs and it gets rid of the rest when you go to the bathroom.

Fun facts:

- It can take more than a whole day for food to move from your mouth to your stomach and through the rest of your digestive system.

- An adult's small intestine is about 23 feet long—that's as long as a garden hose. Your small intestine can fit inside your body because it is coiled up like a rope.

Your Immune System

About: The immune system is made up of organs, tissues, and cells. They work together to protect you from diseases, bacteria, and germs.

Did you know? Your immune system works in several different ways.

First, imagine your body as if it were a castle. Outside the castle there are guards that protect it. Your skin is an example of one of these outside guards. It protects your body so that germs cannot get inside.

Next, if germs sneak past your outside guards, another part of your immune system works to get rid of them by trapping them or pushing them out. When you sneeze or have a runny nose, this part of your immune system is doing its job.

Finally, you have special cells called white blood cells that work together like an army. They patrol your body and destroy harmful germs when they find them.

Your body is SO smart that . . . Your body has a memory. If it finds a germ that could make you sick, it will often create antibodies. These antibodies work along with your white blood cells to recognize and destroy the germ the next time it enters your body.

Fun facts:

- Vaccines that you get from the doctor help your white blood cells fight off certain diseases.

- When you get a sore throat or soreness around a cut, it means that your immune system is working. It's doing its job to get rid of an infection.

Your Nervous System

Main job: To act as the boss and tell your body what to do.

About: This system is made up of your brain, spinal cord, and nerves. It allows you to think, dream, breathe, move, run, laugh, remember, write, sing, smell, taste, and much more!

Your brain is like a telephone operator. Your nerves are like telephone wires that deliver messages to and from all the parts of your body to your brain. Once your brain gets the messages from your nerves, it tells your body what to do. For example, when you want to move your leg, your brain sends messages through your nerves to the muscles in your leg telling them to move.

Did you know? Your brain is what makes you learn, dream, remember, and understand things. Your brain sorts out your feelings and tells you when you are feeling happy or sad. The brain is very complicated. Doctors and scientists are always working to learn more about it.

Your body is SO smart that . . . Your brain is even in charge of things that you don't think about—like breathing or digesting your dinner.

Fun facts:
- Your brain keeps growing until you are about 20 years old. But you're never too old to learn something!

- Human brains are more complex than the brains of any other animals on Earth.

- Your brain weights fewer than 3 pounds.

Your Respiratory System

About: All animals need oxygen to live. Human beings get oxygen from the air we breathe. This system uses the mouth, nose, trachea, diaphragm, and lungs.

Did you know? When you breathe in, air enters your body through your nose or mouth and then travels to your lungs. Your lungs are like two bags inside your chest: They fill up with air and take a part of the air, called oxygen, and send it into your blood. Blood moves throughout your body and delivers the oxygen to every one of your trillions of cells. Cells need oxygen to make energy so your body can work.

Your body is SO smart that . . .
When energy is being made in your cells, a waste gas is also being created. This gas is called carbon dioxide. When you breathe out, your lungs are getting rid of carbon dioxide.

Fun facts:
- Humans breathe in air as oxygen and then breathe out carbon dioxide. Plants do the opposite: They take in carbon dioxide and then release oxygen.

- Every minute, you breathe in 26 cups of air.

- Adults breathe about 23,000 times a day.

Your Cardiovascular System

Main job: To send blood around your body.

About: This system controls the flow of blood in your body. It uses the heart, blood vessels, and blood to deliver oxygen, vitamins, and minerals through the body. It also removes carbon dioxide.

Did you know? Imagine this system as if it were a series of roads. Blood is like the car that travels on these roads. Oxygen, carbon dioxide, vitamins, and minerals are the passengers in the car. One type of "road" is an artery. Your heart sends blood that is carrying oxygen, and other passengers, all around your body through your arteries. Another kind of "road" is a vein. After the cells use the oxygen, they make carbon dioxide and other waste. This waste then gets carried back to the heart and lungs in the blood through your veins. Your heart is the pump that powers this system by pushing blood throughout your body.

Lungs where blood picks up oxygen

heart

Your body is SO smart that . . . This is one of the many systems in your body that keeps running without you even thinking about it. Every minute of every day, your heart is beating and pumping blood through your body. Even when you are asleep, your heart is doing its job.

Fun facts:

● Your heart is about the size of a pear.

● Your heart can pump blood to your feet and all the way back to your heart in 16 seconds.

● Your heart beats about 100,000 times a day.

More Body Systems

Now that you know how amazing your body is, see if you can learn more about some of the other incredible systems in your body, like these: The URINARY SYSTEM cleans your blood and regulates the amount of water in your body. The REPRODUCTIVE SYSTEM allows humans to create babies. The MUSCULAR SYSTEM makes movement possible in your body.

More Body Trivia

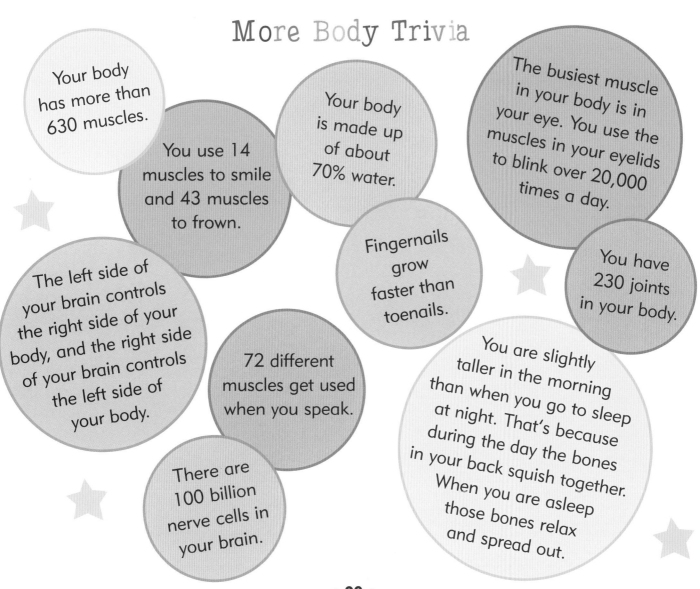

Your body has more than 630 muscles.

You use 14 muscles to smile and 43 muscles to frown.

Your body is made up of about 70% water.

The busiest muscle in your body is in your eye. You use the muscles in your eyelids to blink over 20,000 times a day.

Fingernails grow faster than toenails.

You have 230 joints in your body.

The left side of your brain controls the right side of your body, and the right side of your brain controls the left side of your body.

72 different muscles get used when you speak.

You are slightly taller in the morning than when you go to sleep at night. That's because during the day the bones in your back squish together. When you are asleep those bones relax and spread out.

There are 100 billion nerve cells in your brain.

Being a FRIEND to Your Body

What Does Your Body Need from You?

You've thought about some of the ways your body
takes care of you and makes you happy.

You've also learned a bit about your body's systems and how they work.

**Now it's your turn to think about how you
can be a good friend to your body.**

Your body—just like a machine—needs to be taken care of. Machines
need fuel, maintenance, cleaning, check-ups, and attention.

Your body needs you to be its best friend and take care of it!

Here, you will learn more about what keeps you strong and healthy,
and also about what can hurt your body.

When you know how your body works and what is good or bad for it,
you can figure out the best ways to take care of yourself.

So jump in and figure out some things you can
DO to care for your body and protect it from harm.

Your Body's Needs

Your body needs you to:

Understand it.

For you to care for your body, you need to understand what it needs. That means you learn about how it works, what makes it sick, and what makes it better.

Take care of it.

 Once you know about the things that keep your body strong and healthy, you can do things to be gentle with it. That includes protecting it from harm, helping it grow healthy, and helping it heal or get a little better when it's hurt.

Form healthy habits.

Your body needs you to make healthy choices every day. Over time, these small decisions will become habits. You will see that your healthy choices can make you stronger, smarter, healthier, and happier.

Accept it.

Even when you take care of your body, there can be times that it doesn't work perfectly. Remember, your body is very complicated and amazing and—with your help—it's doing the best it can!

Being a Friend

You have friends and family and other people who care about you.

How do YOU like to be cared about?

I hope that friends and family will: (circle all that apply)

treat me nicely
be respectful of my things
help me get better when I am sick
notice if I feel sad or hurt
BE PATIENT
share with me
have fun with me
protect me from things that could hurt me
APPRECIATE ME
give me attention
be gentle with me
STAND UP FOR ME

You probably circled all of them!

That means that you hope others will take the time to understand you,
be kind to you, and take care of you!

Well, think of your body just like a friend. It needs these same things from you!

 You and Your Heart

Your heart is a muscle inside your chest. It is about the size of your fist. Its job is to pump blood to every part of your body.

Your heart fills up with blood and then squeezes hard to push the blood out and around your body. Your heart fills up and squeezes all the time. As it does this, it creates a heartbeat—the thump-thump in your chest. Your heart usually beats between 60 and 100 times every minute. Your heart also creates a pulse that you can feel on your wrist and neck.

Your heart has four parts—called chambers—that are separated by valves. Valves are like doors that open and close when blood is pushed through them. Your heartbeat is really the sound of the valves closing as your blood is pushed through the chambers.

 Be a good friend to your heart.

When you run around and exercise, your body needs extra energy. To help you, your heart works harder and pumps blood faster so it can deliver the oxygen that your body needs to make energy.

You can tell how fast your heart is beating by feeling your pulse.

After sitting quietly for a minute, ask an adult to help you find and count your pulse for one minute. Put that number here:

Now, run around or do jumping jacks for a few minutes. Then count your pulse again for one minute. Write that number here:

See? You gave your heart a good workout and made it beat faster!

Your heart is just like your other muscles. If you want to keep it strong, you need to exercise it. The best way to do that is to be as active as you can.

You and Your Bones

Bones are really strong so that they can give your body its shape.

Some kinds of food contain a nutrient called calcium that helps your bones to become strong. Milk, yogurt, and some green vegetables are examples of foods that have calcium.

Bones grow long and hard with your help. You can help them get strong by drinking milk, getting enough sleep, and exercising.

Sometimes when you fall or have an accident, your bones can break. When this happens, you might need a cast. Doctors help people when they break their bones, but did you know that your amazing body has its own ways to help repair your broken bones? Your body creates new cells and blood vessels that act like glue to join the broken bones together.

Be a good friend to your bones.

Your bones help you move and also protect your organs.

Fill in the blanks below to find out some ways that you can be a good friend to your bones.

When I ride my bike, I always wear a .... to protect my skull bones and my brain.

I put on my .... whenever I'm in a car to protect my body.

Skateboarding, hockey, soccer, and other sports can be fun. Since I may fall or get hit by a ball playing these sports, I wear pads to cover my .... , ... , and ....

You and Your Immune System

Your immune system spends a lot of energy fighting off germs. Germs are tiny living creatures that are too small to see but sometimes have the power to make you sick. The three main kinds of germs are called *viruses*, *bacteria*, and *fungi*.

Germs can spread through touch. That means that they can be spread when people touch things that have germs on them. Germs can also be spread through the air. For example, when someone coughs, their germs can go into the air that other people breathe.

Most germs don't hurt you. You don't need to be scared of germs because your immune system is very smart, strong, and active. Most of the time, your immune system destroys the bad germs.

Be a good friend to your immune system.

There are lots of ways that you can help your immune system protect you against germs.

- Wash your hands with warm water and soap. It's always good to wash your hands a couple of times a day—especially before eating and after going to the bathroom.

- Cover your mouth with a tissue or your hand when you sneeze or cough. Then be sure to wash your hands.

- Sometimes when you go to the doctor, you get shots. Some shots are called immunizations. These help your body fight off germs.

- Brush your teeth in the morning and at night. This keeps your teeth clean and strong. It also helps get rid of germs in your mouth.

When you do these things, you will be helping yourself and other people by reducing the spread of germs.

You and Your Feelings

Everyone has feelings. We call them emotions. Some days you feel happy and excited. Other days you might feel sad, angry, or scared.

Did you know that sometimes strong emotions can actually make your body feel tired or sick?

Be a good friend to your body and listen to how it feels.

What can you do when you have strong feelings?

Here are some ideas of things you can do to feel better when you are upset. See how many you can find in this word search.

R	S	W	I	D	U
E	K	P	L	A	Y
S	B	R	A	N	B
T	O	U	U	C	E
S	I	N	G	E	Y
S	F	S	H	C	N
T	A	L	K	S	F
R	W	R	I	T	E

WORDS

- WRITE
- PLAY
- LAUGH
- REST
- DANCE
- SING
- TALK
- RUN

If you are feeling down, it often helps if you tell someone.
Can you think of other things you can do to cheer yourself up when you feel upset?

 # You and Your Unique Body

Lots of people have special conditions, illnesses, or reasons that their bodies need special care or attention. Even when people are careful and take very good care of their bodies, they may still get sick or hurt, and it's not their fault.

For example, some people have food allergies. That means their bodies react to certain food in ways that can make them sick. They need to be extra careful about what they eat.

Sometimes a person gets a bad bruise or breaks a bone. While their body or bones are healing, they need to be extra careful.

Some people have diabetes, asthma, or other conditions. They might take medicines or see special doctors.

 # Be a good friend to your unique body.

There might be some times and some ways that your body doesn't work like everyone else's.

If you have an illness or a special condition, what is it?

_____

Can you list three ways that you've learned to be extra careful with your unique body?

1. _____   2. _____

3. _____

Other Ways to Be a Friend to Your Body

Wear sunscreen.
Sunscreen protects your skin when you are outside.

Be kind to your lungs.
You need them to breathe! The best way to keep them healthy is not to smoke cigarettes. Tobacco smoke clogs the lungs and poisons the body.

Your body needs to rest.
When you are sleeping, your body is recharging all the energy it used up during the day. You can help your bones grow, help your immune system stay strong, and even help your brain to think better by getting lots of sleep every night.

Care for your teeth.
Brushing your teeth is smart and good for you. Strong and healthy teeth help you chew your food and talk. Brushing your teeth gets rid of germs.

HEALTHY HABITS
...For a Healthy You!

Here, you can learn more about some things that are good for your health.

Taking care of your body means making decisions each day that will help it to grow, be strong, and be safe.

When you start making these choices all the time, they become **habits**.

Healthy habits are things you can do throughout your whole life to help you stay healthy, active, and happy for years and years!

There are a lot of different healthy habits that you can choose.

This chapter talks about smart and healthy habits that have to do with:
eating | exercise | moderation

You and the Food You Eat

You already know that food gives you the energy you need to make your body run. Food also keeps your body warm, makes you strong, and helps you grow.

To be its healthiest, your body needs the right **kinds** of food and the right **amounts** of food.

Since food is so important to your body, it's smart to take time to learn about healthy eating habits.

Your body needs more of some kinds of foods than it needs of other kinds. It needs lots of fruits, vegetables, whole grains (like cereal, whole wheat bread, and rice), and dairy products (like milk, low-fat cheese, and yogurt). Your body needs smaller amounts of foods like meat, beans, fish, and nuts.

Pretend you are in a restaurant and the waiter asks what you'd like to order.

Circle the choice in each row that you think sounds healthier.

sugared cereal   ~or~   oatmeal

broiled chicken   ~or~   fried chicken

caramel apple   ~or~   an orange

white bread   ~or~   whole wheat bread

bagel   ~or~   doughnut

Some Healthy Eating Tips

BENEFIT FROM BREAKFAST!

Breakfast gives you energy for your day. It can even help you think and do better in school! Some healthy choices for breakfast include low-sugar cereal, fresh fruit, milk, yogurt, whole grain toast, and eggs.

BE ADVENTUROUS.

Your body likes variety. It needs lots of different vitamins, minerals, and fiber. If you eat a mix of different foods, you are more likely to get all of the things your body needs. So go ahead and try new foods, mix it up, and make a balanced diet one of your habits.

SNACK SMART.

Some people like to snack. In fact, eating in between meals is a good way to get energy. Picking smart snacks is the healthy way to go. Try apple slices, carrot or celery sticks, raisins, low-fat yogurt, fig bars, or whole grain cereal.

THIRSTY? DRINK WATER OR MILK.

The healthiest and best way to quench your thirst is to drink lots of water. Other healthy drink choices are milk or 100% fruit juice. Drinks with lots of sugar, like sodas and fruit punch, are not healthy choices for every day.

More Food Facts

Learn which foods are good for you and why.
Here's your chance to do some investigating.

Talk to your family or teacher, or get information from a book or
the Internet, and then fill in the blanks below.

Fresh fruits and vegetables are good for my body because:

....

....

Whole grain breads and cereals provide my body with:

....

....

Milk, cheese, and yogurt all contain calcium, which my body uses to:

....

....

Protein helps my body grow. It also helps build bones, muscles, skin, and blood.
Protein also helps my body repair itself when it is injured. Here are some foods
that contain protein:

....

Here is a list of foods that might
be tasty, but aren't very healthy for
my body. It's okay if I eat them
sometimes, but I know it's smart to
limit how often I eat these foods:

....

....

....

....

What's on YOUR Menu?

Food that's good for you can taste really good, too.
So plan your favorite healthy menu for the day.

Think about what you've learned and write down a balanced menu
that your body and your taste buds will thank you for!

Menu

Breakfast:

Snack:

Lunch:

Menu

Snack:

Dinner:

You and Exercise

One of the very best ways to be good to your body is to give it plenty of exercise.

Your body likes it when you move around and play!

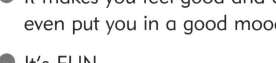

There are many health benefits from
making exercise a part of your everyday routine.

- It strengthens your muscles and bones.

- It gives you energy.

- It helps you sleep better.

- It keeps your heart strong.

- It helps your body to be flexible
so you can move, bend, and stretch
in all sorts of ways.

- It makes you feel good and can
even put you in a good mood.

- It's FUN.

In addition, people who get plenty of exercise are less likely
to become overweight, get sick, or develop certain diseases.

Exercise is good for your body, for your mind,
and even for your happiness.

Being Fit and Having Fun

Being active each and every day is easy when you can choose from SO MANY different things to do.

You can do activities alone, with a friend, or in a whole group. Even if you don't like to play sports, you can still find fun ways to get your heart pumping and stay fit.

• soccer • basketball • running • frisbee • swimming • ice skating • walking your dog • stretching • skating • wrestling • canoeing • golf • tennis • field hockey • tug-of-war • skiing • sledding • martial arts • cheerleading • cricket • baseball • archery • gymnastics • rugby • dancing • skateboarding • cleaning your room • bowling • yoga • jumping rope • doing jumping jacks • biking • playing at a playground • raking leaves • marching • skipping • making a snowman • washing the car • juggling • horseback riding • hiking • watering the lawn • rowing • ice hockey • baton twirling • snow shoveling • walking to school • sit-ups • playing tag • hopscotch

There's not enough room on this page to write down all of the ways to keep your body moving.

The important thing is to find things that you enjoy and then DO them.

Ready? Set? PLAY!

Fill in the answers below.

My favorite active thing to do is:

....

....

....

When my heart is pumping quickly, I feel:

....

....

....

After I'm done exercising, I feel:

....

....

....

Other activities and sports I enjoy most include:

....

....

....

Moderation

Moderation means to have a healthy balance. It is especially good to use moderation in what you eat and the activities you do.

Here are some examples of moderation:

- Spinach is good for you. But if you only ate spinach, you wouldn't get the nutrients that your body needs from other foods. That's why people call a healthy food plan a "balanced diet."

- You know which foods are healthy, but eating treats, like candy or doughnuts, once in a while is okay and won't hurt you.

- It's important to fill your body with food to give it energy. But it's also important to stop eating when your stomach tells you that it's full.

- Exercise is great for your body and your mind. However, if you exercise ALL the time, you won't get a chance to do other things, like learn, rest, or hang out with friends.

- It's smart to wash your hands and brush your teeth. But you don't need to do these things dozens of times every day.

Imagine a seesaw.

Adding too much of something on one side can ruin the whole game.

So, **eat some,** *play some,* REST SOME, study some, laugh some, and be sure to remember the word **moderation** along the way.

SPEAK UP

for Health!

HEALTH ROCKS

You can SPEAK UP for your health by learning about what your body needs. Then you can teach other people what you've learned and take action!

Be a Teacher!

You and your friends can talk to your teacher about learning even more about healthy choices. Then you can do research, write a report about the things you learned, and present it to your class.

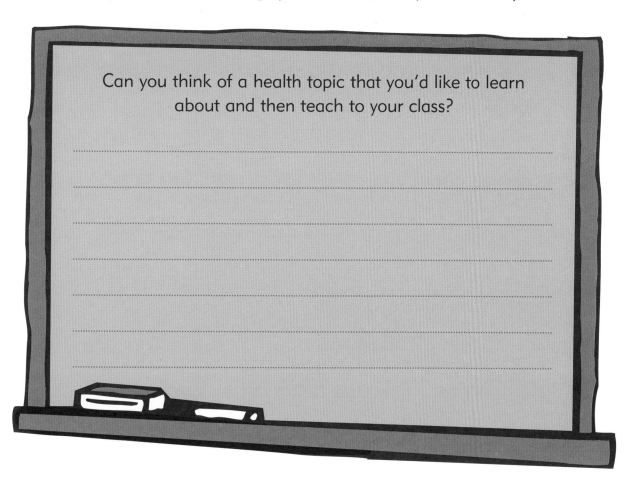

Can you think of a health topic that you'd like to learn about and then teach to your class?

Doctors and scientists are constantly learning more and more about the human body. No one knows everything. But everyone benefits from learning about health. You can even share what you learn with your family.

Show Your Healthy Messages in Your Art

Sometimes people forget to think about their bodies and their health.
You can remind them through your art!

Make a T-shirt and wear it proudly.

My body likes VEGGIES

EXERCISE IS COOL!

I ♥ my heart!

What else can you write on your T-shirts?

You can also share your message through art by making posters, writing poems, or creating songs.

Write a Letter

Here, you can write a note to someone you admire because he or she takes great care of their body. Tell them about why you admire them.

You can write to someone you know—like a family member or friend. Or you can write to someone you've heard about—like a famous athlete.

Dear _____,

_____

_____

_____

_____

_____

_____

_____

From, _____

Think about Some Health Heroes

There are people in your life who do things to keep you healthy
or remind you about healthy choices.

Your Doctor

What is his
or her name?

What advice does he or she give you?

What do you like best about
your doctor?

Your Dentist

What is his
or her name?

What advice does he or she give you?

What do you like best about
your dentist?

Think about the other
people who help you to
be healthy and strong.
You can write about
someone in your family,
a teacher, a coach, a
therapist, or even a friend.

What is his or her name?

What does he or she do that helps you
stay healthy?

What advice does he or she give you?

• 54 •

You Are a HERO, Too!

You've just written about some people who do things to keep you healthy. Well, YOU do things to keep yourself healthy!

Here, you can list some things you do to care for your body.

_____

_____

_____

_____

_____

_____

_____

_____

_____

YOU are a health hero when you take care of your body!

Get Your Family and Friends Involved

When you share your ideas about making healthy choices, you can get other people excited to do the same. Start with your family. Ask them about their ideas on being healthy. Then each one of you can make a commitment to take care of your own body. You can write these ideas down in a "family promise."

Our Family Promise

We each promise to make healthy choices by:

- ....
- ....
- ....
- ....
- ....

Our family's healthy habits keep us strong, active, and happy.

Family signatures:

....

....

Other Ideas

There are so many ways that you can speak up for health and make a difference in your own life and the lives of the people around you!

We know we didn't think of everything.
Here's a page for you to write down some of your other ideas.

....

....

....

....

....

....

....

....

....

....

OTHER STUFF

YAY YOU!

Congratulations!

This **HEALTHY BODY BOOK** certificate shows that you take time to appreciate and understand your body and that you do many things that help keep it strong and healthy.

THE HEALTHY BODY BOOK
This certificate is awarded to

....
WRITE YOUR NAME HERE

for being a good friend to your body.

....
DATE

Now that you know how great it feels to have healthy habits, get out there and keep it up. Remember, you can make healthy decisions each and every day!

Join Watering Can® Press in growing kids with character.

www.wateringcanpress.com

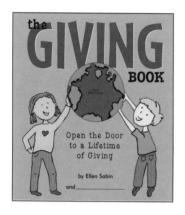

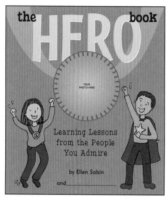

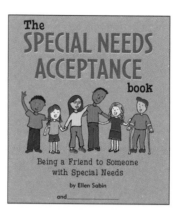

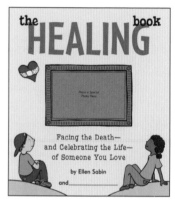

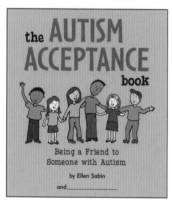

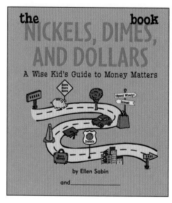

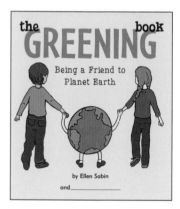

- See other Watering Can® series books.
- Order books for friends/family members or donate copies to an organization of your choice.
- Take advantage of bulk discounts for schools and organizations.
- Learn about customizing our books for corporate and community outreach.
- View the **FREE** Teacher's Guides and Parent's Guides available on our site.

We hope you've learned a lot
about your amazing body
and the healthy choices
you can make every day
to keep it strong and healthy.